MYANMAR

The Land and Its People

MYANMAR

The Land and Its People

Text & Photos by **barry broman**

 **Marshall Cavendish**
Editions

Front cover: Balloon over Bagan pagodas

© 2013 Marshall Cavendish International (Asia) Private Limited

Published by Marshall Cavendish Editions
An imprint of Marshall Cavendish International
1 New Industrial Road, Singapore 536196

Other Marshall Cavendish Offices
Marshall Cavendish Corporation. 99 White Plains Road, Tarrytown NY 10591-9001, USA • Marshall Cavendish International (Thailand) Co Ltd. 253 Asoke, 12th Flr, Sukhumvit 21 Road, Klongtoey Nua, Wattana, Bangkok 10110, Thailand • Marshall Cavendish (Malaysia) Sdn Bhd, Times Subang, Lot 46, Subang Hi-Tech Industrial Park, Batu Tiga, 40000 Shah Alam, Selangor Darul Ehsan, Malaysia.

Marshall Cavendish is a trademark of Times Publishing Limited

National Library Board, Singapore Cataloguing-in-Publication Data

Broman, Barry Michael, 1943–.

Myanmar : the land and its people / text & photos by Barry Broman. – Singapore : Marshall Cavendish Editions, [2013]
p. cm.
ISBN : 978-981-4408-23-3 (paperback)

1. Burma – Description and travel. 2. Burma – Civilization – Pictorial works.
3. Burma – History – Pictorial works. I. Title.

DS527.7
915.91 – dc23   OCN 846751660

Printed in Singapore by Fabulous Printers Pte Ltd

Author's Preface

Despite being the largest country on the mainland of Southeast Asia, Myanmar is the least known in the region and large areas of the country are off limits to foreign travelers. While it is rich in human and natural resources, it is also one of the poorest countries in the world.

But among experts on the region, Myanmar—or Burma as many continue to call it—is considered the hidden pearl of Indo-China. Its rich history and culture, its incredible ethnic mosaic and the charm, wit and friendliness of its people make it a magical place, even in hard times.

Hopefully, these hard times are now changing. This book outlines the tortured history of Myanmar and presents fresh photography of this beautiful country and its many minorities as it moves into a new and happier phase of its history.

It was my privilege to serve in the American embassy in Myanmar in the 1990s. During those years I was able to travel widely and even more so in the years that followed my retirement from government service. I was allowed to visit areas that were off-limits for most foreigners, including several trips into the opium-growing "golden triangle" area of the Shan state, the rugged and chilly hills of the head-hunting Naga hill tribe on the border of India, and the fabled jade mines of the Kachin state. As things change for the better in Myanmar, more of its forbidden places are being opened to the world.

Dedication

This book is dedicated to the memory of
my good friend U Ye Htoon, also known
as Roland. A strong Buddhist, dedicated
husband and father, Roland was a true
patriot who spent years in prison fighting
for democracy for Myanmar. We miss you.

*U Ye Htoon chipping at
his Yangon home*

Acknowledgements

The author wishes to thank the following people for their kind assistance in the production of this book: Claudia Saw Lwin Robert, John Stevenson, Patrick Robert, Sunda Khin, Yuza Maw Htoon, Ma Thanegi, Robert Walsh, Jim Styres, Bob Peterson, James B. Sherwood, Paul Strachan, Yin Min Htay, Neil Hollander, Major General Kyaw Win, John Whalen, U Ko Ko Hlaing, Denis Gray, David Eubank, John Hinchliffe, Swe Swe Mar, Sonny Aung Khin, Robin Markbreiter, and (not least) Betty Jane Apilado Broman.

Myanmar : *The Land and Its People*

For more than half a century, Myanmar was a pariah state. The country known as Burma until 1989 was in the grip of a military dictatorship that brought this resource-rich Southeast Asian nation little but poverty, pain, and fear. The economy collapsed and a series of internal rebellions waged by ethnic minorities and two communist parties wracked the country as it was trying to recover from the ravages of World War II.

"Natives of Burma", 19th century British print

This changed in 2011 when military-controlled elections were held and a general named Thein Sein emerged as president. He was a man of no special note; a staff officer in a regime controlled by troop commanders and untarnished by the excesses and corruption that characterized the military leadership. He quickly began making reforms and brought the country's opposition leader, Aung San Suu Kyi, into a dialogue that led to her winning a by-election in a sweeping victory for her party, The National League for Democracy. The Nobel Peace Prize laureate now has a seat in parliament. Political prisoners were released, censorship of the press ended, and efforts were made to end the long conflicts. Foreign sanctions began to be lifted and hope returned to the land. Thein Sein surprised everyone by giving the people of Myanmar bright expectations for the future after many decades of despair.

Violence has always been part of Myanmar's history, with newcomers constantly challenging older cultures for political supremacy over the centuries. Waves of tribal groups moved into the fertile valley of the Irrawaddy River (now the Ayeyarwady), Burma's great river, usually from the north from Tibet or China. The result was nearly continuous warfare among groups vying for power within the country or against neighboring states. Burma fought at least twenty-four wars against the Kingdom of Siam (now Thailand), for example.

About two thousand years ago, the early Buddhist kingdom of the Pyu people was established in upper Burma along the great river. Little is known about the Pyu, who left ruins that testify to the sophistication and piety of this early civilization. Over time they were supplanted and absorbed by another Tibeto-Burman language group, the Burmans (now Bamar) who migrated out of Tibet about a thousand years ago. But long before the Burmans appeared in upper Burma, another advanced civilization, the Mon, also Theravada Buddhists, had established itself in lower Burma around present-day Bago (Pegu) and Thaton not far from Yangon (Rangoon). The Mon spoke a Mon-Khmer language. Their territory, which extended into present-day Thailand as far north as Chiang Mai, was known in the Indian chronicles as Suvarnabhumi, the "Land of Gold". It was the Mon who built the famous Shwe Dagon pagoda in Yangon, which has become the most important pilgrimage site in Myanmar.

Aung San Suu Kyi having tea with US embassy staff, 1995

In the southwest corner of Burma, beyond the mountains of the Arakan Yoma, another ancient Buddhist kingdom was established at Myauk-U (Myohaung), not far on the Bay of Bengal and modern Bangladesh. The Rakhaing (Arakanese) ruled in isolation for centuries before succumbing to the Burmans in the eighteenth century, when they not lost not only their independence, but also the country's most famous Buddha image, the Maha Muni, which can be seen today in Mandalay.

Another migrating people who moved south into Burma were the Shan, a T'ai-speaking tribe. They moved from Yunnan into northeastern Burma around the same time their kinsmen moved into Thailand, where they eventually supplanted the Mon and Khmer. The Shan encountered the Burmans, and defeated them for a period in the thirteenth century. For much of the past millennium, power in Burma was contested largely between the Burmans in the north, the Mon in the south, and the Shan in the northeast.

Pagodas at Bagan

The Burmans established their first kingdom at Bagan (Pagan) on the site of a Pyu center on the banks of the Ayeyarwady River, about one hundred miles downriver from present-day Mandalay. Their king was Anawratha, who decisively defeated the Mon at Thaton in 1057. The glory of Bagan ended abruptly, when King Narathihapate declined to pay tribute to the Mongol ruler Kublai Khan and foolishly had a visiting Mongol embassy killed. In retaliation, a Mongol army invaded the kingdom in 1287, forcing the abandonment of Bagan and its thousands of temples. Today, it is the premier tourist site in the country.

During the six hundred years following the fall of Bagan, the capital of Burma shifted many times according to the vagaries of war. Power was eventually centered around three cities in upper Burma—Sagaing, Ava, and Amarapura—and finally a fourth, Mandalay, founded in the nineteenth century less than twenty miles from the earlier capitals.

Phaya Gyi temple, Pyu civilization, near Pyay

The first European to visit Myanmar was the Venetian trader Nicolo di Conti, who arrived at Bago in 1435. In 1519 a Portuguese, Antony Correa, arrived at the Mon trading port of Martaban (Mottoma) and tried unsuccessfully to establish trade with the Mon and Siamese further East at Ayutthaya. The first Englishman to record his thoughts on Burma was Ralph Fitch, who dropped anchor in Burma in 1586. He was struck by the great Shwe Dagon pagoda, which was much less grand than it is today. Even so, he called it "the fairest place, as I suppose, that is in the world".

Another remarkable Briton was Samuel White, who, in the seventeenth century, held great power on the lower coast of Burma as a Mandarin of the Siamese court of Ayutthaya. Sam was a freebooter, a man who traded in Eastern waters in violation of East India Company's monopoly. In the eyes of the Company, he was a pirate. He controlled much of the trade on the Andaman Sea from his headquarters at Myeik (Mergui) on the Tenassarim (Thanintharyi) coast, which was ruled by Siam. At a time when few foreigners lived to old age, especially those who incurred the wrath of powerful rulers, Sam was unique. He made it home to Bath in England with his fortune and lived to a ripe old age. But his wife Mary was not so lucky. Her gravestone, noting her death in 1682, can still be seen on the quay at Meek.

King Thibaw, last king of Burma, with his wife and sister-in-law

The Portuguese were active at Myauk-U and sought to establish a trade monopoly in the Arching. Here, they ran into competition with the Dutch, French, and British, particularly the latter who were moving eastward from their base in India. After conquering Krupuk-U and moving westward into areas claimed by the East India Company (a trading company supported by its own army of Indian troops under British officers), the Burmans found themselves in conflict with the Company.

These conflicts gave the British the excuse they sought to start a war with Burma, whose leaders in remote upper Burma had little understanding of the strength of the Europeans. After victory in the First Anglo-Burma War (1824–26), the British wrested the Arian and Tennasarim away from defeated Burma. In 1852, a dispute between Burmese authorities and two British sea captains provoked another military incursion, known as the Second Anglo-Burma War, in which Rangoon and lower Burma were ceded to Britain.

In 1853, King Mindon ascended the throne. He was enlightened by Burmese standards and made an effort to absorb Western ideas, and possessed a better understanding than his predecessors of British capabilities and ambitions. He made the new city of Mandalay his capital, four hundred miles north of Yangon. Although he was a devout Buddhist, Mindon welcomed Christian missionaries and dispatched a diplomatic mission to European courts that included England and France.

Mindon died in 1878 without naming an heir. His successor, Thibaw, was weak and under the influence of his domineering wife, Supiyalat. He secured his position by having many as eighty members of the royal family murdered, not an uncommon practice in Burmese dynastic successions, but an act that repelled and angered the British, who were already concerned over French efforts to gain concessions in upper Burma. The lure of teak forests and ruby, jade, and silver mines seduced the rapacious British and when a British trading company fell afoul of Thibaw, they once again invaded Burma.

The Third Anglo-Burma War (1885) ended Burma's independence. The British Royal Navy—supported by the Scottish-owned riverboat company, the Irrawaddy Flotilla Company—steamed up the river unhindered and trained their guns on Thibaw's teakwood palace. On 1 January 1886, all of Burma was added to Britain's Indian Empire and Thibaw and his family were shipped off to exile in India.

Burmese-speaking Burmans generally live in the lowlands of the country, which are surrounded by rugged uplands and watered by the great Irrawaddy River and its tributaries. The north and west are inhabited by a variety of tribal groups, many of them primitive and usually left alone by the Burmese, as they were by the British. These include the head-hunting Naga in the hills west of the Chindwin River and the Wa, whose homelands are the mountains along the China border in the northern Shan states.

The British ruled the Burmans directly and the ethnic minorities indirectly. If a Burman committed a crime, he went before a British court for judgment. The tribal peoples, in contrast, were ruled by traditional law under the purview of British officials. In the case of the Shan states, thirty-three feudal lords ruled with powers of life and death. Christian missionaries expanded their activities with great success among hill tribes, notably the Kachin and Chin in the north and Kayin (Karen) in the east who had been largely converted by American Baptists since the early nineteenth century. These tribal groups were considered loyal to the Crown and were recruited into British military units while Burmans were not. The British had already fought a bloody guerrilla war against Burmans loyal to their ousted king, and were not about to arm people who might one day fight for their independence.

The British ruled Burma as part of the Indian Empire until 1935 and brought in many Indians to serve in the colonial government and military. Thousands of Indian traders and skilled professional sought better lives in Burma, as did many Chinese

General Aung San and wife

The result left the Burmans a minority in their own capital, Rangoon. Most of the seamen aboard the hundreds of Irrawaddy Flotilla Company boats, for example, were from Chittagong, the major coastal port of Bengal. Hundreds of thousands of Tamils from Madras on the east coast of India were brought to the under-populated Irrawaddy delta to bring in the rice harvest and then returned each year to India, helping make Burma the world's largest exporter of rice before the Second World War.

Like all of the nations in Southeast Asia, Burma was ill-prepared for the Japanese invasion in 1942. Protected by only one infantry division of the Indian Army and a few obsolete aircraft from the Royal Air Force, Burma was quickly overrun. Along with the Japanese came thirty Burmans who had been recruited and armed by the Japanese to form the nucleus of a Burmese military force. This group was known as the Thirty Comrades and was led by a young nationalist named Aung San. His deputy was Ne Win, and together, they founded the Burma Independence Army.

The Allies were quickly pushed out of Burma into India, including a Nationalist Chinese army force under the command of American General "Vinegar" Joe Stillwell. By 1944, the tide was turning against the Japanese as the British Eighth Army under General William Slim returned to Burma, along with Stillwell's Chinese army and Merrill's Marauders, the only American army unit to serve in Burma. Several special operations units such British General Order Wingate's "Chindits" operated behind Japanese lines. The American Office of Strategic Services (OSS), the forerunner of the CIA, recruited more than ten thousand Kachin "Rangers" to harass Japanese supply lines and military outposts far behind the front lines, just as the British Force 136 did with other Burman and minority groups.

The alliance between the Japanese and Burmese nationalists turned increasingly sour, and in March 1945, Aung San took his ten thousand troops across to the Allies. Burma was in shambles by the end of the war, and its economy and infrastructure were destroyed. The British returned to the country, but only briefly. The days of the empire were over. Political parties sprang up, including two communist parties. The ethic minorities were interested in their own independence, not only from the British but also from the Burmans. The leader in the run up to independence was Aung San until he was assassinated by a political rival in 1947.

General Ne Win playing golf in Thailand, 1963

At 4:20 AM on 4 January 1948, an auspicious time selected by astrologers, Burma became an independent country. Its first prime minister was U Nu, a respected nationalist. But the euphoria of freedom from colonial rule was short-lived. At least five armed groups immediately went into rebellion. Many of the veterans of the colonial Burma Rifles were Karen, Kachin, or Chin. The Burma Army under Ne Win fought against more than a dozen armed groups and several of these conflicts have smoldered ever since.

In 1962, Ne Win decided to take the hard-pressed country in a new direction. He led a military coup that overthrew the democratic government of U Nu and announced that he would lead Burma down it's own path to socialism. Businesses were nationalized. The economy spiraled downwards. Human rights suffered and much of the country was in insurgent hands. By 1987, the country that was considered the most developed of all the countries of Southeast Asia before World War II was declared a "least developed country" by the United Nations. That same year, students took to the streets protesting the military regime and Ne Win announced his retirement. The experiment with socialism was dead and the army tightened its grip on the country.

A large demonstration was crushed by military force in August, leaving many unarmed demonstrators dead. A month later, a general election was announced under a multi-party system. This motivated Aung San's daughter, Aung San Suu Kyi, to give up her life as the wife of an Oxford professor and mother of two boys living comfortably in England. She became the leader of the National League for Democracy (NLD).

The NLD won eighty-one per cent of the seats in parliament in the 1990 elections. By that time, Suu Kyi had been placed under house arrest and her party was not allowed to wield the power it had won at the ballot box. Suu Kyi won the Nobel Peace Prize in 1991, but spent much of the next two decades under house arrest. Thousands of her followers were arrested for seeking a democratic government for Burma, which the ruling generals renamed Myanmar in 1990, giving political overtones to the very name of the country.

On the military front, the Burma Communist Party (BCP) self-destructed in 1989 and a ceasefire was announced between the military government and the remnants of the communists, many of them tribesmen under the control of the Wa on the Chinese border. They moved into the drug business but kept their guns, which were mainly used against other drug-trafficking groups. Other ceasefires were signed with the Kachin, Chin, Mon, and other small groups, but not with the Karen or the Shan. The Karen and Shan maintained base camps in or near Thailand, which was happy to have a buffer between themselves and the Burma Army.

International condemnation of the military regime grew in step with the excesses of the generals. Sanctions were imposed and Myanmar was cut off from international institutions such as the World Bank, International Monetary Fund, and the Asian Development Bank. Myanmar became a pariah state shunned by much of the developed world. The military junta's best friend and supplier of weapons was China, ironically the same country that had supplied the BCP during decades of bitter civil warfare.

The surprising reforms by Thein Sein in 2011 created a firestorm of interest in Myanmar, both in terms of economic investment and infrastructure development,

Strand Hotel, Yangon

and international tourism. With the lifting of sanctions by Western nations and Myanmar's return to the world community, its future looks much brighter. But problems still remain, largely with minority groups who still want some form of autonomy as promised at the time of independence. China and discontented generals pushing to regain their influence could make a lethal combination. Democracy is still fragile but the people are optimistic.

Yangon is the largest and most important city in the country. With more than five million inhabitants, this crowded city is still reminiscent of the nineteenth century colonial city that it once was. When it fell into British hands in 1853, Yangon's only claim to fame was the Shwe Dagon pagoda atop Singuttara Hill looking down on the small town. British engineers and planners transformed this backwater of a town into a modern city complete with tree-lined boulevards, parks, and stately colonial office buildings with mansions for the wealthy that included Bamars, Indians, and the British. Rudyard Kipling, the great poet of the Indian Empire, visited Rangoon and stayed at the Strand Hotel, the doyen of Rangoon hotels. He wrote in 1889, "Then a golden mystery upheaved itself on the horizon—a beautiful, winking wonder that blazed in the sun, of a shape that was neither Muslim dome nor Hindu temple… 'There's the old Shway Dagon' said my companion… The

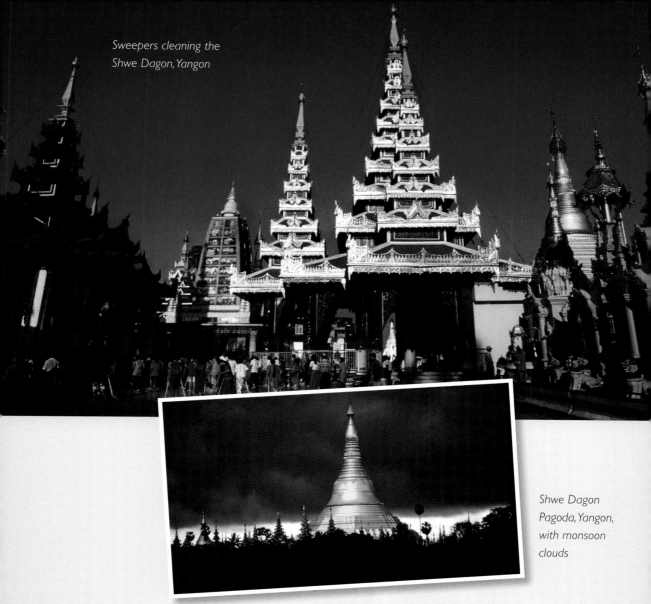

*Sweepers cleaning the
Shwe Dagon, Yangon*

*Shwe Dagon
Pagoda, Yangon,
with monsoon
clouds*

golden dome said, 'This is Burma, and it will be quite unlike any land that one
knows about."

The Shwe Dagon has grown taller and more splendid over the centuries on a
temple site that legend says has been there for more than two thousand years. It
is said there is more gold on the great stupa of the Shwe Dagon than in the vaults
of the Bank of England. It sits on territory that was once called "the land of gold"
and still benefits from solid gold nuggets and dust panned and dredged from the
great rivers to the north.

Women panning for gold in the Ayeyarwady River north of Mandalay

Shwe Dagon Pagoda stupas

The stupa comprises eight thousand six hundred and eighty-eight slabs of solid gold that grow thicker with each re-gilding every ten years. On top of the stupa soars the thirty-foot *hti*, or umbrella, a feature that identifies a stupa as being from Myanmar. More than five thousand diamonds and two thousand rubies and sapphires are embedded in the metal frame of the *hti*, which is crowned by a huge emerald.

Young girl ringing a bell at the Shwe Dagon Pagoda, Yangon

From its humble Mon beginnings, the Shwe Dagon has since been the focus of attention of monarchs seeking to outdo each other with improvements and opulence to gain merit with the Buddha. Queen Shinsawpu, who ruled in the fifteenth century, is remembered for giving the stupa its present size and shape. In addition, she donated her weight in gold to be beaten into gold leaf to adorn the stupa. Given that she weighed ninety pounds and taking into consideration today's gold prices, that is the equivalent of about twenty million dollars in value and a lot of good karma for her majesty.

Wish Granting Buddha image, Shwe Dagon Pagoda

Girl praying at Shwe Dagon

Buddha image under Bodhi tree at Shwe Dagon (the tree is descended from the bodhi tree at Bodh Gaya—see text)

Entrances to the pagoda are guarded by massive *chinthes*, a mythical animal that is half lion and half gryphon. There are four entrances, not counting the newly installed elevator to ease the ascent for tourists and invalids. Shops line the steps of some of the entrances, selling religious items such as images of the Buddha, maroon-colored umbrellas for monks, sandalwood fans, and items for offering to earn merit or have wishes rewarded. People with the latter motivation often approach the Wish Granting Buddha image on the northwest corner of the pagoda's highest level. This is easily identified by the many garlands of flowers that adorn most of the body—gifts from people hoping their dreams will come true. Nearby are two bodhi trees grown from a cutting from the holy tree at Bodh Gaya, India, under which the Buddha attained enlightenment. Merit is also gained by pouring lustral water on marble statues of the Buddha that surround the stupa. Be sure to pour water on the image that corresponds to the donor's birth day of the week.

The faithful making merit at Shwe Dagon

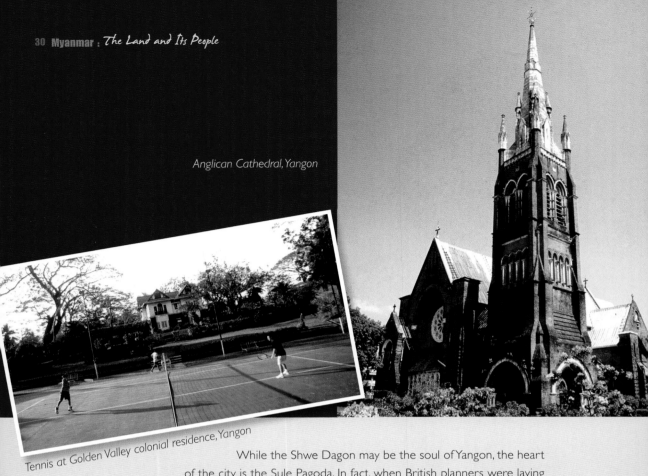

Anglican Cathedral, Yangon

Tennis at Golden Valley colonial residence, Yangon

While the Shwe Dagon may be the soul of Yangon, the heart of the city is the Sule Pagoda. In fact, when British planners were laying out the modern city in a grid system, the Sule Pagoda was placed at the very center of the new town. This elegant, small pagoda next to the town hall is also of Mon origin. It was originally named Kyaik Attok (hair relic pagoda) as it was believed to contain a hair of the Buddha.

Yangon is a melting pot of cultures and today, the many Buddhist pagodas and monasteries share the city with Anglican and Roman Catholic cathedrals, many small Christian churches, Muslim mosques, Hindu and Chinese temples, and even a Jewish synagogue.

Much of the charm of old Yangon relies on its extensive but fast-fading colonial architecture. Because of the economic stagnation that plagued the country for decades, Yangon has been in a time warp. While Bangkok and Singapore sprouted high-rise skyscrapers and eight-lane freeways, Yangon grew older and decayed. Now it may be Yangon's turn to sweep away its architectural heritage thanks to booming land prices and a flood of foreign investment. Some of the civic leaders are trying to preserve the character of the old city, but it is an uphill fight.

Sule Pagoda, Yangon

Governor's Residence Hotel, Yangon

Some grand old buildings have been saved, and even improved on. The old teak Kayah state guesthouse has a new life as the top-rated Governor's Residence Hotel, part of the Orient Express chain. The colonial Bank of India building now serves as the residence of the Indian ambassador. The American ambassador's lakeside residence and surrounding grounds is one of the finest surviving homes from the colonial period.

Residence of US ambassador, Yangon

The venerable Strand Hotel, after years of decline, now soldiers on after a massive face-lift. Some excellent restaurants, such as the elegant haute cuisine Le Planteur with its baroque lounge and the Bamar restaurant Padonmar with its John McCain room for private dinners, are housed in old colonial homes that might otherwise have been torn down.

Padonmar restaurant, Yangon

Le Planteur restaurant, Yangon

Wood carvings at Scott Market, Yangon

Young Buddhist nun at Scott Market

There are many markets in town, but none are better for shopping than the old Boyoke Aung San market, still known to the older generation as Scott Market. This large and rambling market covers two levels and numerous side alleys and has just about everything one could wish for. Generations of Yangon matrons continue to buy their clothing here, from textiles to finished wedding gowns. There are dozens of little shops selling jade and gems. Others specialize in pearls from the southern waters. Antique and craft shops abound as well as art galleries where spirited haggling is expected. Popular items at the moment are tee shirts featuring Aung San Suu Kyi, who is now a member of parliament. There are dozens of patterns to choose from, including a few with American President Obama, the first US president to visit Myanmar. Not long ago, anyone selling, or wearing, such a garment would have been arrested.

Kalaga wall hangings for sale at Scott Market

Yangon fruit seller

There is a new modest National Museum, graced at its entrance by a statue of King Anawratha, who founded the first Bamar kingdom at Bagan. The main attraction is the Lion Throne from the Mandalay Palace. It was removed—looted, some would say—when the British captured King Thibaw's palace and renamed it Fort Dufferin in 1886. The throne and fifty-two other items were brought to England but were returned as a gesture of good will in 1964. The wooden throne is twenty-feet high and heavily inlaid with gold and lacquerware. On top of its historical importance, it is also a major piece of art.

Statue of King Anuratha at the National Museum

Lion Throne, National Museum, Yangon

Getting wet at the Yangon water festival

High pressure hose being used at the water festival in Yangon

Vehicles full of wet celebrants at the water festival in Yangon

If there is a time *not* to visit Myanmar, in my opinion, it is during the Water Festival of Thingyan, a lunar new year celebration held in April. This festival, once calm and quaint, now features a few days of people throwing water from dawn to dusk with great enthusiasm and sometimes more than a little malice. It is a time for the quiet and polite Burmans to let their hair down—and get it wet. I characterize this increasingly rowdy event as the time when the city is divided into two teams; the sadists and the masochists. The sadists throw water, often with high-powered hoses from stands called pendals that spring up overnight all around Yangon, manned by teams of aggressive water throwers and usually sponsored by businesses. The masochist team parades by the pendals knowing they are going to get soaked and perhaps lose an eardrum in the process. Girls put away their skirts or *paso* skirts. Boys leave their *lonngyi* sarongs at home. Out come the blue jeans and Western gear. The cork is let out of the cultural bottle. Business shuts down and traffic is a mess for days. It is a good time to go to the beach.

A one-hour drive from Yangon is the ancient city of Bago, once the thriving capital of the Mon. Heading north, the road passes the British War Cemetery near Hlegu, where 27,000 Allied soldiers from World War II are buried. It is well maintained by the British War Graves Commission. There is another Allied cemetery at the town of Thanbyuzayat in the Mon State, where most of the dead were prisoners of the Japanese working on the infamous Siam-Burma railway portrayed in the film *Bridge on the River Kwai*.

On the outskirts of Bago is the Kyaikpun Pagoda, an unusual fifteenth-century open-air pagoda featuring four Buddha images seated back-to-back in a square. Each figure is about one hundred feet high and faces one of the four points of the compass. Legend says that four sisters took part in the construction of the shrine and if any of them married, one of the statues would collapse. One of the Buddha images was destroyed during an earthquake in 1930, casting doubt on the virtue of one of the ancient sisters.

Allied war cemetery for World War II dead, near Yangon

Kyaikpun Pagoda, Bago

Mahazedi Pagoda, Bago

The golden age of Bago was from the fourteenth to the eighteenth century when the Mon kingdom flourished and initiated trade with the West. Its power extended to Ava in the north in the seventeenth century, but the Mon were decisively defeated a hundred years later by the Burmese King Alaungpaya, who destroyed Bago. With its port silted up and its kingdom gone, Bago became a shadow of its former greatness. Many of its inhabitants fled to Siam where their descendents remain.

Today, the city is remarkable for its many fine pagodas that have been restored. One of these is the Shwethalyaung Pagoda and its spectacular reclining Buddha image that is one-hundred-and-eighty feet long and built in the tenth century. When the city was sacked eight hundred years later, the pagoda collapsed and over time the ruins became a vegetation-covered mound of bricks. In 1889, British authorities discovered that bricks from the long-lost pagoda were being used for a new railway. The pagoda was restored to its former glory and is now a major attraction for both the Buddhists of Bago and a growing number of tourists.

Another site worth visiting is the white Mahazedi Pagoda famed for its challenging steep stairs. It was built in 1560 to house a tooth of the Buddha but, alas, the tooth never arrived. The molar in question had been looted by the Portuguese, who offered it to King Bayinnaung. They were unable to make good on their offer when Catholic authorities intervened and had the tooth ground to powder and thrown into the sea. Despite the missing tooth, the pagoda is impressive and deserving of its name, which means "great stupa".

*Reclining Buddha at
Shwethalyaung Pagoda, Bago*

Porters carrying tourists down from the Golden Rock

Kyaik-tiyo book sellers

East of Bago in the nearby Mon State is one of Myanmar's most famous pilgrimage sites, the landmark Kyaik-tiyo Pagoda and its "Golden Rock". Here, perched precariously on a high ridgeline, a huge gilded boulder with a twenty-four-foot high stupa on top looks as if it might tumble down the mountainside to the sea at any moment. Not to worry, locals say, the stone rests on a hair of the Buddha and is safely anchored. Getting to the rock can be a challenge. It is a five-hour uphill walk from sea level to the stone at an elevation of four thousand feet. A road now shortens the trek, but many pilgrims insist on taking two days to make the journey on foot. For those unable or unwilling to walk to the top, bamboo palanquins and sturdy porters are available for a modest fee to carry passengers up the ridgeline.

Monks at Golden Rock,
Kyaik-tiyo Pagoda, Mon state

*Twante potters
at work*

The road heading west from Yangon leads to the vast and rice-rich Ayeyarwady delta and its nine arms. Improved roads in recent years have made the trip much easier, although it is enjoyable to journey by water to Pathein (Bassein), the main town in the delta. The first town west of Yangon is Twante, a pleasant town with a long-established pottery industry where they make low-fired pots the old-fashioned way. Foot power turns the potters' wheel, a proven method for thousands of years.

In May 2008, the massive Cyclone Nargis slammed into the low-lying delta with such force that whole villages along the coast simply disappeared. More than one hundred and thirty thousand lives were lost. The region is slowly recovering thanks to assistance from outside Myanmar, including the efforts of the Pandaw Charity. When Nargis struck, many roads were washed away so the river-cruise company sent two of their boats into the delta as hospital ships. It continues to assist the recovery of the region, together with many non-governmental organizations.

Buddhist monk in Yangon ducks under a large tree that was uprooted during Cyclone Nargis

Pathein fish seller

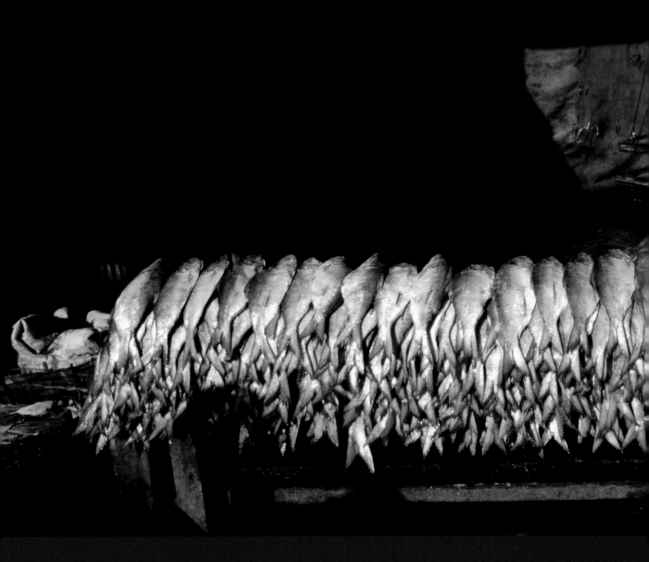

Pathein is a bustling inland center that engages in sea-going shipping. Here, Burmans live in harmony with other groups, including Kayin and Indians. A major local industry is the manufacturing of parasols. A new beach destination an hour west of Pathen is Ngwe Saung Beach, where upscale resorts line the white sand beach on the Bay of Bengal in company with a bevy of more affordable hotels and bungalows. Further up the beach is the more established Chaungtha Beach.

Four hundred miles north of Yangon is Mandalay, the second city of Myanmar and, in many ways, the more interesting of the two. It is the cultural heart of the country. Although the city is less than two hundred years old—an infant relative to the ancient cities around it—and despite being badly damaged in the Second World War, it has fully recovered and is surrounded by older towns that were successively the capitals of the country. Mandalay is the center of most of the country's arts and crafts production, as well as the home of many of Myanmar's largest and most important pagodas and monasteries. Two-thirds of the country's Buddhist monks come from Mandalay.

Ayeyarwady sundown in the delta near Pathein

*Bullock cart on the beach at
Ngwe Saung near Pathein, in the
delta of the Ayeyarwady River*

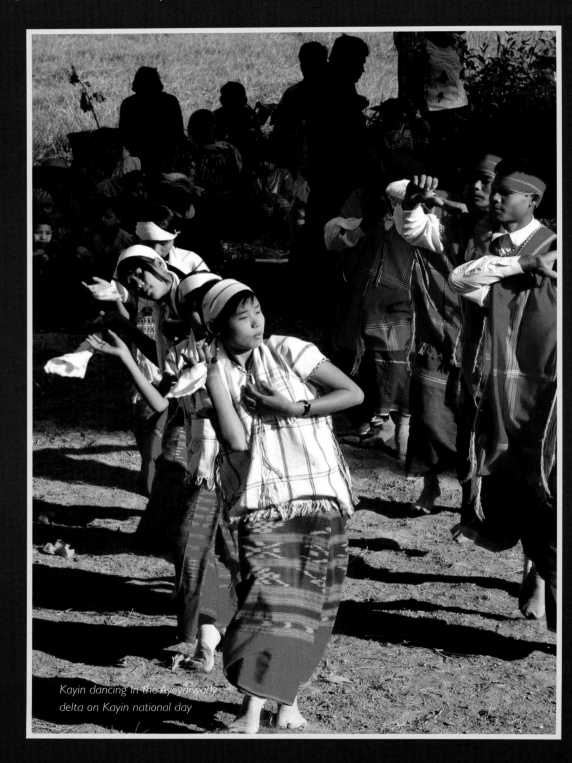

*Kayin dancing in the Ayeyarwady
delta on Kayin national day*

Parasols on sale at Ngwe Saung Beach,
on the Bay of Bengal

Replica of the Mandalay Palace

Mandalay is laid out on a grid with the royal palace in the center, encompassing a square one mile on each side and surrounded by a wall and moat. The city was largely destroyed in 1945 when British forces retook the city from the Japanese and the palace burned down in the process. Today, much of the old palace has been re-created and is open to the public.

The most important religious site in Mandalay is the Maha Muni Pagoda. It was constructed in 1784 to house the great Maha Munha Buddha image that was taken from Rakhaing, following the conquest of the Arakan by King Bodawpaya. The Maha Muni is the most revered image of the Buddha in all of Myanmar. The bronze image stands twelve feet high and was probably cast around the second century of the Christian Era. Crowds of worshippers visit the image daily and the thick layers of solid gold leaf that the faithful have applied over the years has left the image looking bloated to almost grotesque proportions. The face, mercifully, is intact and is washed early each morning.

Moat and wall of the palace in Mandalay

*The image of the Buddha at the
Maha Muni Temple in Mandalay*

An elderly Bamar woman rubs a Khmer bronze at the Maha Muni Temple, Mandalay

One of the most interesting and important collections of ancient bronzes in Mandalay are not of Burmese or even Buddhist origins. They are part of the loot taken from Mrauk-U along with the Maha Muni, and tell the story of the warfare that has characterized the region for centuries. The bronzes are Cambodian and date back to the days of the Khmer empire at Angkor Wat. They were taken by the Siamese in 1431 when they destroyed the Cambodian capital. The bronzes are of Hindu deities and a large three-headed Erawan and are in unusually good condition given their history. They are some of the finest Khmer bronzes anywhere, including their homeland in Southeast Asia. They were later seized from the Thai and brought to Burma where they were in the possession of the Arakanese until taken by the Burmans in 1784. Today, they sit sadly in the back of the Maha Muni Pagoda in a plain room with no identification. They are not ignored, however. Visitors with various afflictions rub the bronze statues on parts corresponding to their ailments, in hopes of finding relief. These large and important survivors of centuries of conflict carry their scars and are in need of repair.

*Woman stroking a Khmer bronze image
in the grounds of the Maha Muni Temple*

A major art form Mandalay is famous for is the *kalaga*, embroidered wall-hangings depicting scenes from Buddhist mythology and themes from the Hindu epic, the *Ramayana*. They are made by artisans of great skill who use colored fabrics, sequins, glass, and sometimes gemstones on a field of velvet. *Kalagas* first appeared in the eighteenth century during the reign of King Alaung-paya. In the nineteenth century, imported velvets and sequins from Europe were used to make them, along with gold and silver threads from India. *Kalagas* are displayed in religious buildings or in private homes. The Mandalay workshop of master craftsman, designer, and artist U Sein Myint is open to the public, as is his private museum next door. A large and beautiful *kalaga* from his workshop is displayed at the United Nations building in New York City, a gift from Myanmar to the UN.

A kalaga *depicting the guardian lion,* chinthe, *from the workshop of U Sein Myint in Mandalay*

U Sein Myint at work on a painting of puppets

Mandalay girl working on a kalaga wall hanging

*Bamar beauty
in Yangon*

Mandalay is the center for the manufacture of religious art for the many pagodas and monasteries in Myanmar. Entire sections on the outskirts of town are filled with foundries that make bronze bells or images of the Buddha. Nearby metalwork ateliers produce the umbrellas that sit atop Bamar stupas. One neighborhood specializes in carving Buddha images out of marble. The former capital of Amarapura—now a suburb of Mandalay—specializes in the detailed and exquisite textiles that Bamar women wear on special occasions.

Young man making a bronze Buddha image at Mandalay foundry

Monks and nuns line up for their one meal of the day at a monastery in Amarapura, not far from Mandalay

Nuns in Mandalay

Marionettes in action in Mandalay

Puppet maker at work in Mandalay

The production of wooden marionettes is another traditional craft in Mandalay. The city has its own marionette theater near the palace, with nightly shows that include dancing and singing along with live music, an entertaining and inexpensive Bamar cultural event. The puppeteers stand in plan view of the audience while manipulating their wooden actors, and the dramas presented are drawn from folk tales and especially from the *Jataka Tales*, which tells of the Buddha's five hundred and fifty lives.

There is a large jade market in Mandalay where stones from the jade mines of the Kachin State are cut, carved, polished, and sold. Since the mines are in a remote area that is off limits to most foreigners, it is a good idea to do your shopping in Mandalay where the prices are the most competitive. Dozens of workshops are in operation while jade dealers nearby display their goods to interested buyers over a friendly cup of tea. Transactions can take hours until a bargain is struck. But before you make a purchase, be aware that jade, just like rubies and sapphires, can have their color enhanced by heat treatment.

Stone carver in Mandalay making
a Buddha image in marble

Inspecting a piece of jade at
the Mandalay jade market

Ruins of the unfinished Mingun Pagoda on the banks of the Ayeyarwady River near Mandalay. It would have been the largest in the world if it had been completed.

*The Mingun Bell, the largest unbroken bell
in the world, not far from Mandalaly*

To visit the massive but unfinished Mingun Pagoda, take a short boat ride up the Ayeyarwady River from Mandalay. Under construction between 1790 and 1797, it was the largest pagoda to ever be built and the brainchild of King Bodapaya, who intended it to house a tooth of the Buddha. The king moved his residence during this period to an island in the river so he could personally supervise the a work force of thousands of slaves, many of them taken during the conquest of the Rakhaing. But poor economic conditions prevented the completion of the ambitious project. Work was halted and the king died in 1813, leaving behind a hundred and twenty-two children, none of them interested in renewing the construction work. A major earthquake in 1838 damaged the unfinished pagoda, causing a huge rent down the middle of the three hundred and thirty-three-foot high structure. Finished or not, the pagoda still makes an impressive sight from the river.

Despite not managing to complete the Mingun Pagoda, Bodapaya did achieve one construction record. He produced the world's largest unbroken bell, the famed Mingun Bell which may be seen, but not rung, near the pagoda. The massive bronze bell weighs eighty-seven tons and stands twelve feet high. The bell was cast in 1790 for installation at the Mingun Pagoda. It is still waiting.

Pwin-U-Lwin (Maymyo) stage coach taxi

Pagodas on Sagaing Hill look
down on the Ayeyarwady River
and Mandalay beyond

Silver image of the Buddha in a
Sagaing silversmith's workshop

*Inwa (Ava)
ferry boat near
Mandalay*

The former capital city of Sagaing sits just across the river from Mandalay at the Inwa (Ava) Bridge, one of the very few that spans the great river. It was destroyed in 1942 by the retreating British army to delay the Japanese, and was not rebuilt until 1954. The main feature of the town is Sagaing Hill, an imposing high ground filled with pagodas and monasteries offering excellent views of the river, Mandalay, and the Shan hills to the East. Sagaing is noted for its silversmiths who operate dozens of workshops in the town, continuing a long tradition of excellent craftsmanship. Another former capital, Inwa, rests on lowlands near the river and is cut off from road traffic during the monsoon season. Vestiges of its greatness still remain, including an old watchtower and some fading pagodas. Public transport in the town is mainly by pony cart, especially when the river intrudes.

An hour east of Mandalay and up on the Shan Plateau is the old British hill station of Maymyo, which in Burmese means May's town, in memory of a British army colonel in the late nineteenth century. Now renamed Pyin U-Lwin—its original name— this charming town sits at an altitude of thirty-five thousand feet, providing relief from the stifling heat of Mandalay amid pine trees and lush gardens, an arboretum, and golf course. Among the many attractions of this hill town are the mini-stage coaches that form an ecologically friendly taxi service.

The pine forest is dotted with old English-country-style houses, once the summer homes of the Raj. Some have been converted into bed and breakfast-style inns. Among this group is the famed Candagraig, built in 1905 by the Bombay Burma Trading Company for its timber officers as a "chummery" where they could relax en route when returning from the teak forests of the north. The name was given by the company's Scottish owners in memory of a famed manor house in the highlands of Scotland. Generations of travelers to Myanmar have sought out the Candacraig, which is known for its roast beef and Yorkshire pudding dinners. My wife and I were the only guests when we first visited the small hotel in 1994. It had fallen on hard times and instead of a menu they asked what we wanted for dinner and we enjoyed a very tasty chicken curry and fresh vegetables. After dinner we moved outside to the verandah for a quiet cigar and Scotch whiskey to enjoy the sound of a light wind wafting through the sheltering pines. Out of the dark a man approached. He stopped and saluted. He was the night guard, an old Gurkha who had stayed on after the war. I greeted him in Gurkhali and he continued his rounds.

Candacraig Hotel, Pyin U-Lwin

Thanbodday Temple near Monywa on the Chindwin River

Spires of the Thanbodday Temple

Traveling West from Mandalay across the river and driving south takes one to the relatively new (it was built in 1939) and unique Thanbodday Temple built in an architectural style reminiscent of Borobodur on Java, the largest Buddhist monument in the world. This magnificent complex consists of a central temple with a series of terraces, each of them hosting a forest of small stupas. There are said to be more than five hundred thousand images of the Buddha in this remarkable temple.

Crossing the Chindwin River at Monywa near Thanbodday on a Z-Craft ferry is an adventure in itself. The boat is patterned after a World War II landing craft with a bow ramp to admit passengers, buses, automobiles, and bullock carts. Fifteen miles from the river is the ancient archeological site of Pho Win Daung. Thousands of Buddha images are in the Shwedaq Taung temple complex, including many carved out of the rock walls of the caves in situ. The walls and ceilings bear well-preserved mural paintings in this "dry zone" of upper Myanmar that includes Bagan and Mandalay. The temple also features a huge white elephant carved in the sandstone rock face entrance to its cave. Inside, more than four hundred thousand small images of the Buddha are placed on niches carved out of the cave's walls.

Images of the Buddha at the Pho Win Daung Cave near Monywa

Rock carving of an elephant at the Shwe Ba Daun cave temple near Monywa

*Thousands of images of the Buddha
at the Thanbodday Temple*

While most Bamars are followers of Theravada Buddhism, many also follow an older—and darker—tradition. This is the pre-Buddhist belief in spirits or *nats*, as they are known in Myanmar. The cult of *nat* worship is built around thirty-seven *nats*, each of which were once humans and all died violent deaths. They all have followers who propitiate the spirits to keep them happy and also to ask for favors that they believe the *nats* can grant. In addition to the thirty-seven main *nats*, there is also a *nat* of automobiles known as Yoke Ka So. Many motorists starting out on a road trip from Yangon stop at the Shwe Nyaung Bin shrine located next to a bodhi tree by the road to have their car blessed to ensure a safe journey.

A nat kadaw *dancing to please the* nats *at the Taungbyon* nat *festival near Mandalay*

Images of The Mother Buffalo Nat *on sale in her hometown, Bago*

There are *nat* festivals held annually throughout the country. One takes place at Taungbyon, a town not far from Mandalay, where thousands of people gather each year to pay tribute to two brothers, the Taungbyon Brothers, who were killed in the eleventh century by the king of Bagan and who are among the thirty-seven *nats*. Small gilded wooden images of the sword-wielding brothers are stored in a shrine throughout the year and brought out for the nine-day festival in their honor.

Image of one of the Taungbyon nats about to be paraded before the faithful at the Taungbyon fair

Offerings to the nats at the Taungbyon nat festival

Shrines for nats in Golden Valley, Yangon

Statues of the two Taungbyon brothers being carried through the crowd at Taungbyon

Blessing a car at a nat *shrine near Yangon before beginning a long journey*

Woman praying before nat *images at the Shwezigon Pagoda, Bagan*

The mediums who can speak to the *nats* are called *nat kadaws* or "honored wives". Many of them are transvestites and they communicate with their *nats* by dancing and drinking themselves themselves into a stupor with Mandalay rum or Johnny Walker Black label whiskey, depending the budget of their patron who underwrites the event. The objective is to please the *nat*, who is believed to have the power to grant wishes. Conversely, *nats* can be malevolent so it is a good idea to keep them happy. The king of the *nats* is Thagyamin and his home is on Mt. Popa, the 5,000-foot-high core of an extinct volcano thirty miles East of Bagan that is considered the home of the *nats*. Like the Taungbyon brothers, *nats* are often favored regionally. The Buffalo Goddess *Nat* Bago Mai Daw, for example, is honored around Bago and is known by her water buffalo horns.

Although *nats* are not part of the Buddhist religion, the two are linked. Sule Bo Bo, for instance, is the guardian spirit of the Sule Pagoda in Yangon and is also

View of Shwezigon Pagoda, Bagan, from a balloon

the protective spirit of Singuttara Hill, the site of the Shwe Dagon Pagoda. Also in Yangon, the Nat Phone Shein Pagoda is dedicated to *nats* but also houses Buddha images. When King Anawratha sought to promote Buddhism among his *nat*-worshipping people at Bagan in the eleventh century, he built the Shwezigon Pagoda but was careful to include *nat* images in the shrine in an effort to guarantee acceptance of the Buddhist images, which are still worshiped at the Shwezigon.

Any trip to Myanmar is not complete without a visit to Bagan. Over the Bagan plains, on the banks of the Ayeyarwady River, stand as many as two thousand pagodas and stupas in varying stages of decay, although massive restoration efforts in the past decade have brought a halt to the decline. At its zenith, as many as six thousand religious structures were thought to be in Bagan, on top of the thousands of wooden buildings (including palaces) that disappeared long ago. An estimated one third of the lost pagodas fell in the Ayeyarwady River as it changed its course over time.

Bagan's most important building is the Ananda Temple. Completed in 1091, it is considered the masterpiece of Mon architecture. It is said that King Kyanzitta was so moved upon seeing the finished work that he personally executed the architect so that the temple would not be replicated. Not a very Buddhist thing to do, but typical of the mores of Burmese royalty. The temple stands 104-feet-high, with four vestibules that each contain an image of a standing Buddha crafted in gilded teak. Every year, an Ananda Temple fair attracts many thousands of Bamar, many of whom arrive by bullock cart and stay for days.

Bagan is much larger in size than its contemporary Angkor in Cambodia, which experienced a similar fate. Stupas dot the Bagan Plain and are best seen from a hot air balloon. From a field near the Shwezigon Pagoda, balloons seek a breeze that will carry them over the pagodas and away from the river.

Ananda Pagoga, Bagan, from a balloon

Shwesandaw Pagoda, Bagan

Stucco detail from the Ananda Pagoda, Bagan

*Cattle grazing among
the temples of Bagan*

*Dhammayangyi
Pagoda, Bagan*

The largest temple at Bagan, the Dhammayangi, has a dark history. King Narathu, having murdered his father, wanted to atone for his sins and believed that by constructing the temple, he would achieve merit. He wanted its workmanship to be without equal and personally supervised the builders. Legend says that if the king could slip a needle between the building stones, the workman responsible would be executed. The policy was hardly calculated to encourage good labor relations, but it did ensure that this temple is the best constructed of all the great structures of Bagan. It probably did not help Narathu's karma, however. He was assassinated and the temple was never completed.

Bagan has two guardian *nats*, a brother and sister, who take station in niches flanking the Tharabar Gate in the wall of the old city. The brother is The Lord of the Great Mountain and his sister is Lady Golden Face and their mission is to protect the thousands of Buddhist shrines around them.

Many of the pagodas and temples at Bagan were constructed by Mon architects and workers who were among the thirty thousand prisoners taken during the fall of Thaton. One of these temples was the Manuha, designed and paid for by the Mon king, who was himself a captive. It contains four Buddha images, all of them in very cramped quarters, perhaps reflecting the distressed state in which the former monarch of the Mon found himself.

Man praying at the
Manuha Temple, Bagan

Lady Golden Face,
a nat guarding
Tharabar Gate,
Bagan

Bagan-style paintings for sale, Bagan

The prototype of all Burmese stupas is the Shwezigon Pagoda built by King Anawratha that stands close to the banks of the river. It is the most important reliquary shrine in Bagan and was a part of his campaign to further the Buddhist religion. Among the relics he acquired were some bones said to belong to the Buddha and an emerald image of the Buddha from China. Today, the pagoda has been beautifully restored in hues of gold and red.

Bagan is the center of the lacquerware industry in Myanmar, continuing a tradition that is centuries old. It takes weeks and several intricate steps to produce lacquerware, which is often used in Buddhist rituals. *Hsun-oks*, for example, are receptacles used to carry food to monasteries as offerings to the monks. They are often made of lacquered wood but can also be constructed from split bamboo. An array of practical applications of the art are found on boxes, cheroot containers, incised cups, trays, and drinking cups. The finest of the latter are made from horse hair, producing an object of incredible flexibility. In Yangon, this craft has been taken to new heights by Patrick Robert Associates (PRA), the brainchild of expatriate Frenchman Patrick Robert and his vivacious Shan wife, Claudia Saw Lwin. The company creates a wide array of original and often bizarre arts and crafts that are world class, both in terms of design and production.

Lacquerware hsun-oks, receptacles for carrying food to monestaries

A large gilded lacquerware creation from PRA

A large lacquerware creation
under construction at the PRA
workshop in Yangon

PRA gallery at Golden Valley, Yangon

A wicker motorcycle, one of the many eccentric and magnificent creations at PRA

Claudia Saw Lwin with daughter Belle Robert at their home in Yangon at the showroom and gallery of Patrick Robert Associates fine art and crafts products

Not far from the ruins of Bagan is the town of Naung-U, home of the Bagan airport and river port. It is full of shops, an expanding market, food stalls, and lodging for budget travelers. Visitors with deeper pockets should seek out hotels along the river banks such as the vintage Thande Hotel, whose main building was built for the one-day visit of the British Prince of Wales in 1922.

Getting around Bagan is easy. There is rarely any traffic pressure on this spread-out archeological site with its widely-dispersed pagodas. Bicycles are available for rent, as are cars with drivers, but the most evocative and "green" method of transport are the pony carts that quietly ply the unpaved lanes leading to the beautiful historical structures.

Lacquerware for sale at Nyaung-U near Bagan

Bagan pony cart

Perhaps the best way to arrive in or depart from Bagan is via the traditional method—boat. There are a number of options, starting with the Orient Express flagship, The Road to Mandalay. This former Rhine River cruise ship features a swimming pool and red-carpet service throughout. More traditional boats for these waters are the Pandaw boats patterned after the teak-fitted vessels of the old Irrawaddy Flotilla Company that once traveled these waters in the days of the Raj. The Pandaw boats have shallow draft that enable them to navigate the tricky and shifting channels of the Ayeyarwady and Chindwin rivers.

Swimming on the Road To Mandalay cruise boat

Enjoyng a drink on a Pandaw cruise boat's sun deck

A Pandaw boat coming into a river town

*Left: Girl selling
thanakha wood at
Sagaing*

*Right: Applying
thanakha cosmetic*

First-time visitors to Myanmar will soon notice that many Bamar women wear a distinctive cosmetic on their faces. This is *thanakha*, the product of the *thanakha* tree (*limonia accidissima*), whose bark is ground into a powder and mixed with water to form a paste that is applied to the face, often in patterns designed to express individuality and/or attract the opposite sex. This unique, natural, cooling, and fragrant make-up allows women and girls (even some boys and men) of Myanmar to enjoy flawless skin while making a fashion statement at the same time. Children of both genders often have their entire bodies covered by a light thanaka application, especially in the hot season.

Legend says that *thanakha* was first used by a princess as early as the second century of the Christian Era. It first appears in literature in a fifteenth-century poem and was a fixture in the royal courts where favored princesses were allowed to mix their *thanakha* with pure gold leaf. In the eighteenth century, King Alaungpay

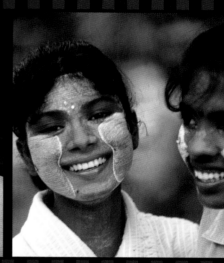

owned his own *thanakka* forest for the exclusive use of his royal ladies. *Thanakha* trees once grew wild, but demand for their bark is such that plantations now fill the need from the thin, crooked, trees that grow to around twenty feet in height. The best soil for this healing tree is found in the dry zone of upper Myanmar, near the town of Monywa. While purists grind their own powder from small rounds of the tree on a stone slab, it is often easier and quicker to buy factory-made powder or cakes of *thanakha*.

Women working outdoors often apply a thick paste of *thanakha* as a form of sunblock to protect their skin from the tropical sun. This versatile product is not only used by Bamar women—minorities such as Indian, Chinese, and tribal ladies enjoy this iconic product. While there are many arboreal products from teak to rosewood available in the country, none is more vital to the ladies of Myanmar than the humble, stunted, yet potent *thanakha* tree.

Left: Pathein road construction worker with thick thanakha *on her face to protect her skin from the sun*

Center: Mandalay girl wearing thanakha

Right: Yangon girls of Indian heritage wearing thanakha

Parliament building, Nay Pyi Taw

Uppatasanti
Pagoda,
Nay Pyi Taw

The newest city in Myanmar is both the nation's capital and the fastest growing city in the world. This is Nay Pyi Taw, located two hundred miles north of Yangon. Construction began in 2002 and it was named the new capital in 2005 at a time when all foreigners and most Bamar were not allowed to go there. It is already the third largest city in the country, a sprawling urban setting of wide boulevards, graceful parks, and a massive parliament building built on an almost deserted avenue at least twenty lanes wide. Nearby is the Uppatasanti Pagoda, a scale replica of the Shwe Dagon in Yangon and built to house a gift from China said to be a tooth of the Buddha. Nay Pyi Taw is still very much a work-in-progress and many Bamar and most diplomats in Yangon are reluctant to relocate there. But there are good hotels at very reasonable prices, an excellent toll road linking it to Yangon in the south and Mandalay to the north, and a new golf course.

One of Nay Pyi Taw's spectacular successes is its large and well-designed zoological garden. Unlike the old Yangon zoo where the animals are confined to cages, this new zoo is mostly open-air in complete harmony with the jungle-clad hills outside the park. Exhibits include an albino Bengal tiger, gibbons swinging from towering trees, and an unusual, igloo-shaped white structure housing five penguins who live in air-conditioned comfort.

Myanmar is the largest country on the mainland of Southeast Asia, covering more than two hundred and sixty thousand square miles of land and with a population of more than fifty-five million people. From north to south, it stretches more than thirteen hundred miles from the icy mountains of bordering Tibet to the tropical rain forest lapped by the Andaman Sea. The country is administratively divided into divisions and states. Generally, the majority Bamar—who make up about sixty per cent of the population—live in the low-country divisions while

Penguin house, Nay Pyi Taw zoo

the ethnic minorities reside in the upland states along the border with India in the west, China in the north, and Thailand to the east. Dozens of tribal groups live in the hills, including the famed "long neck" Padaung women, the fierce head-hunting Naga, and the heavily-armed and opium-growing Wa.

The Shan State bordering both China and Thailand is the country's largest state. The Shan are a T'ai-speaking people closely related to the Thai. They migrated South out of China a millennium ago and settled in the river valleys of northeastern Myanmar, where they practiced wet-rice cultivation and Theravada Buddhism. In the late thirteenth century, the great King Mengrai founded the city of Keng Tung (Kyaingtung) in the Shan state and Chiang Mai in northern Thailand. The Shan fought many wars with the Burmans over the centuries and, for a brief period, controlled all of upper Myanmar with their capital at Sagaing near Mandalay.

Gibbon in Nay Pyi Taw zoo

The late Sao Sai Long Mengrai, the last sawbwa of Keng Tung, the largest of the Shan states

Under colonial rule, the Shan state was divided into thirty-three smaller states each ruled by a feudal lord called a *sawbwa*, who wielded power under the benign watch of the British. This continued after Myanmar's independence in 1948, with many of the minorities looking forward to greater autonomy as promised by the new constitution. The power of the *sawbwas* ended abruptly in 1962 when the army seized full power. Some of the Shan leaders were killed, others imprisoned, and the rest fled. The last feudal lord of Keng Tung was the late British-educated Sao Sai Long Mengrai, a direct descendent of King Mengrai. Educated at Kings School in Canterbury during the Battle of Britain, he was relocated to Australia where he remained for the duration of World War II. He liked to be called by his nickname, Shorty. When the army gained power, he was imprisoned for six years. After his release he was prohibited from leaving Myanmar and was not allowed to reside in Keng Tung. He was eventually allowed to leave the country. He returned late in his life but was rarely allowed to visit his home in the Shan state lest he foment unrest. Shorty died in Yangon in 1997.

Several Shan political organizations joined other minorities in insurrection against the Bamar. One was the Shan State Army, which still remains in opposition today. Another group, The Mong Tai Army, claimed to be Shan nationalists in ideology but were, in reality, a drug-dealing gang led by a Sino-Shan named Chang Ch'i-Fu who called himself Khun Sa. Under pressure from the army in the 1990s, he surrendered his army of more than ten thousand men and went into retirement. That left the door open for his main competition in the drug business, the United Wa State Army, to take over.

Wa soldiers buying raw opium, Wa Hills

Rice paddies in the Wa Hills

The Wa are a tough minority group living in the rugged and remote hills along the China border in the northern part of the Shan State. They were called the "wild Wa" by the British, who never tried to bring the war-like tribe into the colonial fold. Opium cultivation under the British was encouraged for sale to Chinese, and export and production was taxed and strictly controlled in areas under British control. George Orwell's father was an opium tax official in India, a fact that might have colored the writer's outlook on Burma, especially after his service as a colonial police officer. Most of the opium production by the Raj was in India and aimed at the China market to redress the trade imbalance caused by the British desire for Chinese tea and silk. A solution of sorts was found in the sale of opium to China, but the the Chinese did not want it to come into their country and cause instability and great human misery. This led to the Opium War in 1839, which ended in the humiliation of the Chinese and the cession of Hong Kong island to the British, who proceeded to flood China with opium.

With Myanmar wracked by civil war after 1948, it was easy for remote warlords to organize the opium trade in the mountainous regions that came to be called the Golden Triangle. Most of this trade was in the hands of ethnic Chinese, including remnants of the Nationalist Chinese army who sought refuge in Myanmar and Thailand after being defeated by the communists in 1949. Opium had been grown in the area for many generations, but the drug trade became more sinister, deadly, and profitable after heroin became the main product.

The Wa Hills in morning fog, heart of the Golden Triangle

Late in the nineteenth century, scientists at the German pharmaceutical company Bayer invented a new opium-based, pain-relieving drug. They trademarked the drug and named it Heroin. It was ten times more powerful than opium and much easier to transport. It was also much more addictive and was eventually outlawed. That did not stop the drug lords of the Golden Triangle—at one point ninety per cent of the world's opium was produced in jungle laboratories and smuggled around the world. The Wa became the leading heroin-producing gang in the world, operating from a large region they call the Wa State, and boasting an army of around thirty thousand tribal fighters.

Palaung tribesman smoking opium, Wa Hills

Opium fields from the air, Shan state

Lahu girls scoring opium poppies, Wa Hills

Casinos at Mong La, on the Chinese border in the northern Shan state

Many of the Wa and their tribal allies had been foot soldiers in the Burma Communist Party in a bitter war against Myanmar that was supported by the Chinese government. When the party collapsed in the late 1980s, the Wa signed a ceasefire agreement with the Bamar and kept their weapons, increasing their drug business in an area known to the Bamar as Special Zone 2, into which the Myanmar army would not enter. Another Special Zone under the control of a former communist leader was also located on the China border. Its main town, Mong La, was a major tourist destination for Yunnan residents, who were drawn to the casinos, brothels, and bars that made it a "Las Vegas in the jungle". The city has a museum dedicated to the abolition of narcotics in the area, and an anthropological theme park featuring some of Myanmar's tribal folk in a sort of "human zoo".

*Palaung women
in the Wa Hills*

Palaung women, Wa Hills

Kachin girls helping to burn opium poppies in Lashio, Shan state

*Lahu mother and child celebrating
Lahu New Year, Wa Hills*

Hotel built of bamboo on pilings
in Inle Lake, Shan state

Due to ongoing insurgencies and the dangers of traveling in drug-producing areas, much of the Shan State near the border of China is closed to tourism. Many other areas are open and the number of sites that welcome foreigners is growing. The chief tourist attraction in the Shan State is Inle Lake, a sixty-square mile shallow body of water in the southern part of the state. This is the home of the Intha people, a group that migrated to the lake in the eighteenth century to escape fighting in lower Myanmar. They are an industrious people who produce much of the country's tomatoes, cucumbers, and other vegetables on floating gardens.

*Catholic cathedral at
Lashio, Shan state*

Selling crafts from boats on Inle Lake

The fishermen of Inle Lake have a unique method of moving their small boats. They wrap one leg around a long oar to propel their boat while standing on the other leg. They fish with long conical gill nets that trap their prey on the bottom of the lake, which is just ten feet deep at its deepest point. The lake is a major tourist destination and the latest hotels are constructed of bamboo on stilts over the lake, as are many of the residences in the area and a few famous Buddhist monasteries. A good place to shop in is at the floating market nearby—among the crafts on sale are textiles woven by Intha women.

There is a small community of Padaung at the lake. They moved from the nearby Kayah State to escape a long running civil war of the Kayah, who are cousins of the Kayin. All of the Kayah State is off limits to visitors. The Padaung are known for the brass coils that some of the women and girls wear around their neck. Legend says that a king once visited the Padaung and fell in love with a Padaung maiden, whom he made wear the constraining and heavy brass coils as a means of making her unattractive to other men. Others say the coils were put on the women to ward off slave-takers. The practice is now dying out, but the Padaung girls and women at Inle Lake make a good living from having their photos taken with tourists, for a fee.

Padaung "long neck" woman with brass rings on her neck being photographed with Chinese tourists in Mong La

Paduang girl washing her neck rings, Kayah state

Intha man rowing his boat with a leg at Inle Lake

Mining rubies at Mogok,
Shan state

Tiger Tunnel into the Bawdwin mine. Herbert Hoover killed a tiger on this spot in 1914.

Bawdwin silver mine, Shan state

A difficult place to visit in the Shan State is the remote mountain town of Mogok, home of the finest rubies in the world, particularly the 'pigeon blood' rubies deemed the best of the best. Rubies are mined in open pits with high-pressure hoses blasting the red clay hills to get at the gems, which also include sapphires. Mogok has been mined for centuries. Outsiders are forbidden to buy or trade gems at Mogok, where rubies are bought and sold quietly by small groups of traders. All gems purchased by tourists must come from government licensed shops in Yangon or Mandalay.

Anther mining area in the Shan State is the famed Bawdwin silver mine located in the northern part of the state not far from China. It has provided silver to China since the Ming dynasty which ended in 1644. The mine is owned by the government and employs thousands of people who mine and smelt not only silver, but also lead and zinc. Early in the twentieth century, a young American mining engineer was hired by the British to try and improve production at the mine. He succeeded and made a fortune. This was Herbert Hoover, who later became president of the United States. In 1914, he had a tunnel drilled into a mountainside to connect to a deep shaft. He called it the Tiger Tunnel because he shot a tiger on that site. It is still in use, as is some of the mining equipment that Hoover bought, but the tigers are long gone. A narrow gauge-steam-powered train connects the mine with the nearby smelter at Namtu.

A field of ancient stupas at Kakku, Shan state   *Pa-O girl guide at Kakku*

South of Taunggyi, the capital of the Shan State, in an area controlled by the Pa-O people, is the archeological site of Kakku. This area was off limits for years due to the insurgency of the "Red" Pa-O, who are now at peace with the government. Kakku, a pleasant drive from Taunggyi through rolling hills and many garlic farms, features a forest of old stupas, some dating back to the eleventh century. There are said to be more than five thousand stupas, some of them in an advanced state of decay. The effect is striking. There is also a good restaurant at the site with an excellent view.

South of the Shan State is the Kayin (Karen) State which abuts Thailand. Much of the border region is closed to tourism due to conflict with the Karen National Union (KNU), the longest running civil war in the world. While there is a ceasefire in effect, there are still many internally displaced persons struggling for survival in the jungle. Thousands of Kayin have fled to Thailand where they live in large refugee camps and some have been there for decades. Many suffer from malaria or the aftermath of encounters with land mines.

Rebels of the Karen National Union rest at a forward position near the Thai border in the Kayin state

Many Kayin are Christians. In 1813, the first American female missionary arrived in Myanmar. She was Ann Judson, the wife of Adoniram Judson who converted thousands of Kayin to the Baptist faith during his thirty-seven years in the country. Judson also established several schools—many Kayin are very well educated. Judson College in Yangon later became part of the University of Yangon. Many Kayin were recruited by the British as soldiers and the head of the army was a Kayin at the time of Myanmar's independence. Soon after the British left, the Kayin went into rebellion, along with other minority groups. At one point, they captured both Mandalay and the Yangon airport. The level of conflict is low these days and there is hope that after sixty years of war, the new regime in Nay Pyi Taw will sign a permanent peace agreement.

Kayin refugee at a camp in Thailand with his father, who lost a leg to a landmine in Myanmar

Kayin girls in Yangon
in national dress

Kayin wedding party in Yangon   *Kayin refugees in Thailand*

Part of the Kayin State has been opened for tourism, including the state capital of Pa'an located on the banks of the fast-flowing Thanlwin (Salween) River. Near Pa'an is the incredible Kawgun Cave, where Mon Buddhists carved thousands of small Buddha images on the cave walls centuries ago. Inscriptions date the earliest images to be from the seventh century and it appears that the cave has been a site of worship ever since. There are larger, more modern Buddha images in the cave and a few monks serve as caretakers. Some looting has taken place but many of the carvings are high up the cave walls, making them relatively safe. Hopefully, better security for these sacred objects will be provided as more people discover this ancient site.

Thousands of Budddhas at Kagun Cave

*Carvings of the Buddha on
Kagun Cave near Pa'an*

Egrets near Pa'an

East of Pa'an is a beautiful Buddhist monastery resting on an island in a small lake. It features a high piece of limestone karst rising abruptly out of the island, festooned with stupas that can be reached with the help of long, fragile, bamboo ladders. It is a test of faith to scale this rock formation. Nearby is another monastery where monks lovingly care for a great field of seated Buddha images lined up in long rows.

An oasis in the conflict along the Thai Myanmar border is the town of Myawadi, a major crossing point over one of the few bridges on the border and a major trading center. Here, tourists can leave the Thai town of Mae Sod to enter Myanmar for the day for a small fee, without the need for a visa. Those who do not want to cross the bridge and pay the fee can try to cross the Taungyin (Moei) River on large inner tubes under the noses of Bamar border guards.

People crossing illegally into Thailand near Myawaddy, Kayin state

Pagoda on limestone karst near Pa'an

Forest of eastern Kayin state near Thailand

Kayin girl going to harvest rice, Kayin state

Buddhas in a row, Kayin state

The remote Kachin State covers much of northern Myanmar in steep, sparsely-populated mountains bordering Tibet. The highest point of Myanmar is Mount Khakaborazi, thought for many years to be unclimbable until an intrepid Japanese expedition scaled the mountain for the first time in 1996. The main ethnic group in these hills—from which rise the Ayeyarwady and Chindwin rivers—is the Kachin, which includes numerous sub-tribes of the main Jingpaw Kachin tribe. Other tribes in the hills include the Naga, Rawang, and Lisu.

The Kachin are fierce fighters and were highly sought by the British as soldiers for the Burma Rifles. A battalion of Kachin accounted themselves well under British officers in World War I while serving in Mesopotamia. Originally animist, many Kachin were converted to Christianity by American Baptist missionaries in the nineteenth century and churches great and small dot the landscape. During the Second World War, Detachment 101 of the American Office of Strategic Services, forerunner of the CIA, recruited ten thousand Kachin Rangers. They harassed Japanese lines of communication, provided intelligence, and rescued downed Allied airmen flying "The Hump" from India to China over hostile terrain.

Like other minorities, the Kachin went into rebellion after independence but signed a ceasefire in 1993. In 2011, the Myanmar Army broke the ceasefire and fighting resumed. As a result, travel to the state by tourists was severely curtailed in 2013. The best jade in the world comes from an area around the town of Hpakant along the Ulu River West of Myitkyina, the state capital. Off limits to most foreigners, this area provided emperors of China with their coveted "stones of heaven" for centuries. Chinese mining companies have been allowed into the area and have damaged the environment and badly depleted jade stocks with thousands of laborers using heavy equipment and explosives, further straining relations with the Kachin.

Geis Baptist Church in Myitkyina, Kachin state, made from river rocks from the Ayeyarwady River

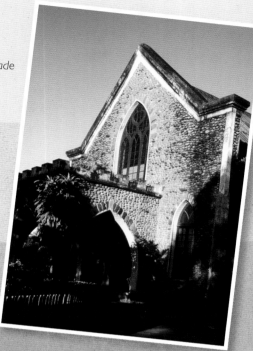

Lone river boat moving down the Chindwin, Nagaland in background

Once the conflict and depredations end, the Kachin State would make a perfect venue for eco-tourism. Trekking companies are already taking hikers into the pristine forests where rhododendrons can grow up to forty feet high. Many of the rhodies sold in the West today come from seeds collected by the British botanist Kingdon Ward during his expeditions into the Kachin mountains early in the twentieth century.

Jade rock for sale in Yangon

Kachin jade miners at Hpakant

White water rafting near Putao, northern Kachin state

Bamboo raft floating down the Chindwin river

Monks receiving their meal for the day at Mindat, Chin state

Kachin girls north of Lashio, Shan state

A rustic yet elegant Malikha Lodge is located near Putao, the northern-most town in Myanmar, offering thatched bungalows with huge wooden hot tubs and Finnish wood-burning stoves. A small Western staff provides gourmet cuisine and a staff of Lisu tribesmen and women provide excellent service. Whitewater rafting on rivers that eventually form the great rivers of Myanmar is available to the truly adventurous. More sedate visitors can do their eco-trekking on the backs of elephants. The state is home to the largest tiger reserve in the world, which can be found along the old Ledo Road that American engineers built in 1944 from Ledo in India to Myitkyina, through malaria jungle in the Hukwang Valley.

Eco-tourism on elephant back near Putao

South of the Kachin State lies the small Chin State along the border of India. The Chin, who call themselves the Zo people, were largely converted to Christianity in the nineteenth century and were also recruited into colonial military units. They, too, were in rebellion for much of the past sixty years. Although the guns are still in the Chin Hills, tourism is now allowed. The Chin are a friendly people with a long tradition of making tightly woven textiles, tattooing women's faces, and playing the nose-flute.

Kachin woman's skirt made of wool

Facial tattoo on a Chin woman, Mindat

Chin boy playing a flute with his nose

South of the Chin state is the Rakhaing state that is boxed in by the Bangladesh border, the Bay of Bengal, and the mountains of the Arakan Yoma. The ancient Rakhaing civilizations pre-date the arrival of the Bamar and maybe even the Mon further east. It is the youngest and most remote of the states and is proud of its long status as an independent kingdom. Its capital, Sittwe (Akyab), sits at the mouth of the Kaladan River which leads upstream to the old capital of Mrauk-U, once the center of power on the Bay of Bengal and original home of the Maha Muni sculpture now languishing in Mandalay. Today Mrauk-U sits in ruins, a ghost of its former greatness.

Row boats at work in Sittwe harbor, Rakhaing state

Fishing village at Ngapali Beach, Rakhaing state

Although predominantly Buddhist, the Rakhaing State and, in particular, its capital Sittwe, has an Islamic flavor thanks to its colonial history and proximity to Bangladesh. Over generations, a minority population of Muslim Rohinya have emigrated from Bengal, to the chagrin of the state and national governments. The economic outlook for this oft-ignored state is bright, thanks to the discovery of natural gas offshore. A pipeline to China promises a boom time for this poor but scenic part of Myanmar. Much of its beauty lies in the broad, sandy, palm-lined beaches of Thandwe (Sandoway), along the Bay of Bengal coast south of Sittwe and easily accessible by air from Yangon.

Perhaps the most interesting, but little seen, minority group along the Indian border is the Naga. This Tibeto-Burma group consists of numerous sub-groups all answering to the name Naga, but with different traditions and tribal dress. They are perhaps best known for their custom of taking heads, a practice that put them in direct and long-standing conflict with British colonial administrators. While the Kachin and Chin were determined to be ideal martial material, the Naga were considered too primitive to wear a uniform and wield modern weapons. Most Naga live on the Indian side of the border, which is loosely demarcated by the spine of the Paktoi Mountain range. The Indian Naga are heavily Christianized and much studied. The Myanmar Naga (who may number one hundred thousand

Naga dancing with raised dah (knife), Layshi, Nagaland

Makuri Naga men arrive at new year celebration in Lahe

today) were left to their traditional practices of head hunting and slave taking. Old British maps define the Naga hills as "unadministered territory" with no roads and few trails. Today. the Naga hills west of the Chindwin River are generally off limits to foreigners. The Naga live much as they always have, hunting forest animals such as sambaur, wild boar, and monkeys. They feast on the meat of semi-wild mithan buffaloes washed down with home-brewed beer. Rivers yield three-foot long carp and upland rice and many crops are grown on steep hillsides.

In recent years, a few tourists have been allowed into the Naga hills to attend Naga New Years celebrations, the brainchild of the Ministry of Tourism. Naga New Year is somewhat like a gathering of clans in the Scottish highlands a century ago. Thankun, Makuri, Konyak and other tribes meet for several days of feasting on mithan, drinking home brew, and dancing around huge bonfires at night in the cold winter air. The straight-laced Myanmar army hands out tee shirts to the bare-breasted women and soccer shorts to the loincloth-clad men as they walk into camp, sometimes after a trek of seven or eight days through the mountains.

The Naga are a proud and independent people who take great pride in their personal appearance. The headdress of the men tell of the animals in the forest. Tigers are fast disappearing, but their claws still adorn male helmets, along with bear and monkey fur, wild boar tusks, hornbill horns, and feathers. If a creature is dangerous or edible the Naga will kill it, usually with muzzle-loading home-made guns. The ladies are equally fashion-conscious with their woolen bodycloths, silver jewelry, cowrie-shell and bead necklaces, and facial tattoos. These annual gatherings afford the clans a chance to meet, trade, party, and arrange a few marriages.

One of the most esteemed products of Myanmar is teakwood, grown in remote mountains that still contain seventy-five per cent of the world's reserves. In areas controlled by the central government, teak cutting is carefully restricted along the lines laid out by British teak companies that were extracting timber even before Britain ruled Myanmar. Central to Myanmar's teak industry are its elephants. These ecologically friendly and cost-efficient animals drag the felled trees to heavy trucks or to streams where they can be floated downstream to mills. They tread lightly on the land, doing minimal damage to the environment (avoiding the need for roads, for example). There are almost six thousand elephants working in the forests of Myanmar, some privately owned, others civil servants. Another thousand roam free in the jungle.

Naga headdress with hornbill horns and feathers, bear fur, and wild boar tusks

Heimi Naga girls showing off her silver jewelry, Lahe, Nagaland

Llainong Naga girls pounding rice at Lahe

Young teak forest near Pyay

Working elephant in the Pegu Yoma

Working elephants work eight hours a day, sleep eight hours a day, and feed eight hours a day. They begin their timber-hauling career at the age of fourteen, the same age as their *mahout* (handler), or *oozy* as they are known in Myanmar. The two form a team throughout their careers and retire together at the age of sixty. An elephant working for the Myanmar Timber Enterprise learns twenty-four voice commands and does their best work in the monsoon season when heavy rains provide plenty of water for the pachyderms and the streams that carry the logs to market. In the hot months, both elephants and their human partners relax in mountain camps on rest and recreation, waiting for the rains that will signal the resumption of work in the hills.

Feeding an orphan elephant near Toungoo

Another remote and long-ignored area of Myanmar is the long, narrow strip of land and islands that make up the Thanintharyi (Tenassarim) Division. This stretch of land along the Andaman Sea and the eight hundred pristine islands of the Mergui Archipelago form a tropical paradise with everything in abundance—except people. Completely undeveloped and with few residents, this area was once part of Siam and the first point of the British into the Myanmar. Its main town, Myeik (Mergui), was a vibrant trading center.

The area has tremendous potential, particularly in the development of off-shore oil and natural gas. An existing gas pipeline transports gas into Thailand. The potential for tourism is huge: diving enthusiasts have already discovered the "Burma Bank", an offshore diving paradise in the waters of southern Myanmar where groups from Thailand are allowed in to scuba-dive from live-aboard boats. There are hundreds of heavily forested, virtually uninhabited islands with white sand beaches and fish-filled seas waiting for tourists to discover.

Activity in Myeik (Mergui) harbor, southern coast of Myanmar

*Moken people, also known as sea gypsies, ashore during
a the monsoon season in the Myeik Archipelago*

Sea gypsies (Salon people) are a nomadic and primitive group who live aboard fragile boats and ply the islands wearing few clothes and living on delicacies such as sea worms. During the monsoon season that dumps hundreds of inches of rain on the coast in a few months, the sea gypsies live on land.

Myanmar is a part of Asia that time seems to have forgotten. Tigers still roam the high country in diminished numbers, although travelers have more to fear from malarial mosquitoes than large carnivores. The country is in a period of transition between the modern world and traditional society of the past, where village monasteries once provided educations, electricity and modern medicines were rare, and modern amenities and democratic government were unheard of. The change is happening very quickly, and people who wish to see how Myanmar was in the days of Rudyard Kipling need to act quickly.

About the Author

Barry Broman served as counselor of embassy at the United States embassy in Yangon 1994–1996, at which time he retired from government service. He earned a Masters of Arts degree at the University of Washington in 1968 and served as an infantry officer in the United States Marine Corps for three years, including service in Vietnam. He has written and photographed numerous books on Myanmar subjects, as well as produced four documentary films on the country. His most recent book in this series was *Cambodia: The Land and the People*. He resides in Kirkland, Washington with his wife Betty Jane. He is pictured with Daw Aung San Suu Kyi in Yangon in 1995.